To all the wonderful lyricists who
gave meaning to my life.

Philip Springer

Composer Philip Springer

The last legacy of
E.Y. "Yip" Harburg

I am Phil Springer, a songwriter from New York City, now living in California. I am fortunate enough to have been chosen by the great lyric writer, E.Y. "Yip" Harburg, to be his final collaborator. I would like to share with you the story of our collaboration. We wrote about 15 complete songs together, and I have chosen 10 of them for this presentation.

Yip Harburg and I met in 1950, when I was 24 and he was 54. It was a cool October day. I went to his apartment at 25 Central Park West, in NYC, and knocked on his door on the 8th floor. A lovely middle-aged woman took my arm and led me in to where the great sandy-haired lyric writer was sitting on a chair. We said hello and exchanged greetings. We both knew that I would be at the piano so Mr. Harburg did not waste any time in motioning me towards his little spinet piano where I sat and played him eight songs. I played songs that I had written for the Columbia College Varsity show, most of them from a show called "Streets of New York" which was produced at Columbia University in 1948. I also played Mr. Harburg one or two melodies which I had written when I was in the dormitories in Columbia and had a piano in my room, which was a rarity as a student at Columbia College.

That first meeting lasted about two hours and it shaped my entire life. I became part of the inner circle of Yip and Eddy Harburg; playing the piano at all of their parties, accompanying Yip, who loved to sing his own songs; that was always the high point of the evening.

Early in our friendship, Yip gave me the nickname "Flip". When we first met, he said to me, "Flip, when we write please don't think about what I have done and what you have done. Think of us both as beginners, working together." Still, it turned out that we really did not write much together in the years after that first encounter. One of the reasons the collaboration did not work all those years was because I was always so in awe of this man whom I revered; I almost froze at the piano. It was difficult for me to relax and have fun, which is needed in song writing collaboration.

But Yip's words remained in my mind and only came true 22 years later. In 1972, Yip came from New York to California, called me and expressed a great interest in working with me. I was, of course, honored, so I agreed. Knowing that he needed me made me feel very relaxed with him and, for the first time, I was able to write music in his presence. This opened the doors to Yip and I working nine years together happily, easily, productively and I hope, greatly.

Yip Harburg to Philip Springer:
"Flip, when we write please don't think about what I have done and what you have done."

"Knowing that he needed me made me feel very relaxed with him and, for the first time, I was able to write music in his presence."
Philip Springer

E.Y. Harburg and Philip Springer. (1980)

"I realized that the greatest lyricist of our time wanted me to be his composer. So naturally, I was very honored."
Philip Springer

Music by
Philip Springer
Lyrics by
E.Y. "Yip" Harburg

1 It Might Have Been
Cole Razzano

6 Change of Sky
Claire Birmingham

2 Edelaine
E.Y. "Yip" Harburg

7 Love Comes In Many Different Colors
New York Background Singers

3 Hitchhikers
E.Y. "Yip" Harburg

8 Drivin' and Dreamin'
Alan O'Day

4 Wild Red Cherry River
Philip Springer

9 Almost
Glenn Rosenblum*

5 Time, You Old Gypsy Man
E.Y. "Yip" Harburg

10 Crazy Old World
E.Y. "Yip" Harburg**

All songs: piano accompaniment by Philip Springer

* The recording of "Almost" was produced as a home demo, not pretending to be near state-of-the-art recording. Despite the quality of the tape, the composer chose this version because of the soulful performance which he found far more moving than other professionally produced recordings of this song.

** Performance at 92nd Street Y, NYC, January 1980

All songs co-published by Tamir Music and Glocca Morra Music Corp. (ASCAP)

Philip Springer

1940

1947

1990

1978

E.Y. Harburg

1978

1930

551 Fifth Avenue, New York, N. Y. 10017

October 24, 1977

Mr. Philip Springer
Pacific Palisades, Ca. 90272

Dear Phil:

I have been thinking about the revue, which sounds more and more exciting as it develops. I do hope you will not keep thinking of this as a one woman show or lead Paula Kelly to start thinking along these lines only. One woman and one man shows are dangerous. There is too much to uphold for an evening, and I have seen too many of them go wrong with the greatest of comics. We must keep thinking of this as Paula Kelly with a group so that we can get variety, and the songs we already have will get full value.

Some of your envisioned electronic devices are brilliant and can work three or four times throughout the evening, or maybe more, but there must be more faces on stage to hold an audience for the whole evening.

If we keep talking of a one woman show, she may become obsessed with the idea and it will be hard to change.

I am sending under separate cover some songs and will keep digging more up as we go on. I will be in the Vineyard for the next two weeks. My address is Box 181, Chilmark, Mass. 02535. My telephone number is 617-645-9404.

As always, it was inspiring to see you.

My best,

Yipper

per B

EYH:sb

9

YIP

⑩

G. Gershwin

1 It Might Have Been

The collaboration of the first song on this album started at that first meeting with Yip. I played what I thought was the strongest melody I had composed that was the closest to the music of a man that Harburg (and I) worshiped, George Gershwin. After he heard the melody, Yip sat down and started writing a lyric on a yellow legal pad, as I watched:

*It might have been a
different tale
But love's a breeze and
I'm a sail
And who am I to question
my lot
Love being what it is*

And then he said, "I apologize for writing Love with a capital L, but I do it because I've made so much money on that word."

We did not finish the song that day. And then, perhaps twenty years after Harburg's death, I finished that melody. And to my amazement, it fit the lyric that Yip had given me to go home and write on the day of our first meeting.

*The waning moon
The rose that withers
All too soon*

*If love must fade
It's part of the plot
Love being what it is*

*Since you wandered by
Like a firefly
Leaving me your glow for
awhile*

*What is to be said
Now the glow has fled
Love was mine to know
for awhile
Just for awhile*

*If tears could talk
And words could weep
If splintered hearts
Could only sleep*

*I might forget
The way you forgot
Love being what it is*

2 Edelaine

Yip wrote the lyric to "Edelaine" as a paeon to his wife Eddy. The song has a great significance in the history of our 30-year relationship.

Before I talk about that significance, a few thoughts on the age-old question, when writing a song: "Which comes first, the music or the lyrics?" In the Brill Building era, I wrote with many great lyric writers and found that there are a few ways in which you could write together. It was exceedingly rare, in my career, that songs began with the completed lyric or a completed melody. Most songs begin with the title. A few begin with a short musical phrase. Others might begin with a few lyrics. If the other partner likes it, they start a "back and forth" process, inspiring each other with lines and music.

"Edelaine" was the first song where Yip and I found our rhythm in working together. Up to that point, from 1950 to 1972, the way Yip liked to work was for the composer to write a complete melody, to which he would then write a lyric. I was not into that way of creating and consequently it was only rarely that I came in with a finished melody, and Yip would then write a lyric to it.

The writing of "Edelaine" was different. For the first time, Yip gave me the title and a line: "If you have once met Edelaine, you shall not find repose again". That phrase inspired me to write the first part of the melody, and that tune inspired Yip to write his next line: "For no matter where you run from star to sun, from sun to star, She will be there infallible as spring". We completed this song in that way, back and forth, and from then on, for nine years, we had an easy-going relationship where I could compose freely and he could write freely.

E.Y Harburg and Edelaine Roden Harburg

Edelaine

If you have once met Edelaine
You shall not find repose again

For no matter where
You may dare to run
From sun to star
From star to star

She will be there
Infallible as spring
To wake every living thing

Edelaine, Edelaine
Are you wind, are you song, are you rain?
In every leaf, her laugh, her sigh
Will break your heart
Or light your sky

Every rose you touch
Every road you turn
Will bring her back with thoughts that burn

You'll fly haunted by her face
To find peace in some you embrace
What has your kiss
Meets that new kiss
You will find your heart whispering this

If you have once met Edelaine
You shall not find repose again
You shall not find repose again
Repose again

3 Hitchhikers

The story of "Hitchhikers" comes in three chapters. The first is when I played this tune to Yip in the spring of 1973. As I played it, one of us came up with the title "Hitchhikers" and we both knew immediately that the melody felt right. From there, we started running lines:

Out on that highway
Lonesome and wide
We are only hitchhikers
Thumbing a ride
Headed for somewhere
Out of the strife
Out on that highway
The highway called life
On that highway called life

Headed for somewhere
Out of that night
Out of the darkness
Into the light

The next line hit me like a sledgehammer. I could hardly believe what I was hearing:

Learning the secret
That cuts like a knife
That somewhere is nowhere
On that highway called life

I said, "Yip, are you saying that life has no meaning?" He did not answer me. I asked if he could change that line; he did not.

Chapter Two occurred five years after Yip's death. I met with a professor of poetry at The Berklee College of Music in Boston, Massachusetts and we discussed my collaboration with Yip, and the song, "Hitchhikers". I told him I was troubled about that line in the lyric. The professor said that was Mr. Harburg's dark vision. That is what he wanted to say, and you cannot tamper with it. I knew that he was right, and that discussion ended that chapter.

Chapter Three occurred decades later, when I took out the song again. I finally finished the song, with only a few needed adjustments. The recording here is Mr. Harburg reciting that lyric about two years before his death, with music and background added when I finished the song.

So, brother driver
Why pass me by?
Your way is my way
On that highway called life

Out on that highway
Lonesome and wide
We're only hitchhikers
Lonesome hitchhikers
Thumbing a ride
Thumbing a ride

"The professor said that was Mr. Harburg's dark vision, that is what he wanted to say."

4 Wild Red Cherry River

In October 1978, in New York, Yip Harburg called and said "Phil, come over, I want to show you some lyrics." I went to his beautiful apartment at Central Park West and 86th Street. The sun was setting over the Hudson River and the view of Central Park was gorgeous.

Yip greeted me and showed me a composition book, one of those black and white books, with about 80 pages. Every page was filled with a lyric. He looked at it for a moment and then shook his head as if to ask, "How will I ever write all these songs?" I knew what he was thinking, and I said "Yip, let's just write one... show me a lyric that you would like me to write music to". And he turned the page to a lyric called "Wild Red Cherry River" and took a photograph of that page for me to work on. Here is a photograph of that original lyric that Yip showed me. I took it back to my place, worked on it for a couple of days, came back and said "Yip, here's what I came up with; I hope you like it."

"WILD RED CHERRY RIVER

music Phil Springer   lyric E Y Harburg

Quiet

THERE'S A WILD RED CHERRY RIVER
THAT WAS ONCE A GENTLE STREAM
FLOWING CALMLY DOWN A THOUSAND LITTLE LANES.
NOW IT'S WIDER THAN A LONGING
AND IT'S DEEPER THAN A DREAM
IT'S THE WILD RED CHERRY RIVER IN MY VEINS.

I CAN FEEL IT LEAPING TOWARD YOU
TOWARD THE HARBOR OF YOUR SONG, SILENT
LEAPING OVER LITTLE GRIEFS AND STRONG PAINS.
THERE'S A WISDOM IN ITS MADNESS
THAT KEEPS SWEEPING ME ALONG
ON THIS WILD RED CHERRY RIVER IN MY VEINS.

FIFTY YEARS OF RUSHING TOWARD YOU
THROUGH THE BRIGHT DAYS AND THE DARK
FIFTY WINTER SNOWS AND FIFTY SUMMER RAINS
ARE CUT DEEP INTO THE PASTURES
OF THE VALLEYS OF MY HEART
BY THAT WILD RED CHERRY RIVER IN MY VEINS.

AND THE WONDER OF IT ALL IS
HOW THE PASSION OF IT GROWS
WHILE THE MEASURE OF ALL OTHER TREASURE WANES.
HOW MY EYES WON'T SEE YOU OLDER
WHILE THE LIGHT WITHIN THEM GLOWS
LIKE THE WILD RED CHERRY RIVER IN MY VEINS.

THERE'S A GLORY IN A HUNGER
FOR A SONG THAT'S STILL UNSUNG
AND A LOVE THAT LIVES FOR LOVELIER REFRAINS.
PEOPLE SAY..."YOU'RE LOOKIN' YOUNGER"
BUT I'LL ONLY BE AS YOUNG
AS THAT WILD RED CHERRY RIVER IN MY VEINS.

WHAT IT MUST BE LIKE IN HEAVEN
HEAVEN ONLY SEEMS TO KNOW,
BUT WHATEVER HEAVEN IS THE THOUGHT REMAINS--
CAN IT BE MORE THAN THIS LOVE IS,
OR PERHAPS THE OVERFLOW
OF THAT WILD RED CHERRY RIVER IN MY VEINS?

"Wild Red Cherry River", original lyric typed by E.Y. Harburg

17

5 Time, You Old Gypsy Man

Yip publicly stated that "Time, You Old Gypsy Man" was his greatest song. Yip premiered and performed this song at his "Lyrics & Lyricists Series" show at the 92nd Street Y in New York City in January 1980. I am honored to have composed the music.

Yip and I were working together on a summer evening in 1979, around midnight, following one of the renowned Harburg parties. Yip had given me the title, "Time, You Old Gypsy Man". I played for him what I created upon hearing the title. When he heard the music, tears came to his eyes and he said, "That's what I was looking for all my life." It took us about two evenings, both after midnight, to complete the song.

TIME, YOU OLD GYPSY MAN
Music by PHILIP SPRINGER
Words by E. Y. HARBURG

LOOK TO THE RAINBOW
A MUSICAL

THE LIFE & LYRICS OF E. Y. HARBURG

Devised & Directed by Robert Cushman
Stage & Choreographed by Dennis Grimaldi
Production Musical Director Michael Dixon
Designer Glenn Willoughby

Starring JACK GILFORD

with: Michael Cantwell
Isabelle Lucas
Mandy More
Barbara Rosenblat
Simon Russell Beale

Time, you old gypsy man
Thief on the wing
Drugged me with rhapsody
Tricked me with spring

Fiddled me off my feet
Danced me on air
Sprinkled my daydreams
with gold dust
Then silvered my hair

Silvered my hair you rogue
Crinkled my eyes
Whistled the bird of youth
Out of my skies

Time, you old vagabond
Riddle me this
What did you do with
Forever and ever
That sealed every kiss

You packed up your
tambourines
Stilled your guitars
Slipped off into the night
Turned off into the stars

Stripped me of song and
spring
Robbed me of rhyme
Fled in your carnival caravan
But you old gypsy man
Thanks for a glorious time!

"'Time, You Old Gypsy Man' is a little-known masterpiece."

New York Times, December 10, 1989
Review by Stephen Holden

6 Change of Sky

I regard "Change of Sky" as Yip's and my masterpiece. I feel that "Change of Sky" reached a far greater emotional height than our other songs. Director Barry Kleinbort expressed his opinion that "Change of Sky" is the closest I have come to writing a tune in the style of Harold Arlen. And since Arlen is one of my heroes, that compliment meant a lot to me. I consider it an art song as well as a jazz song.

"Change of Sky" was recorded by a leading jazz singer in England, Tina May. She also named the album "Change of Sky."

In the Spring of 1980, Yip came to me with the title. He had already tried to work with other composers to find the melody but had no success. He asked me, "Would you try?" I played a melody that I felt fit the title and Yip loved it. I finished the melody that afternoon. Yip took it home, spent a few days with it, and wrote the extraordinary lyric. The poetry, imagination and the sensuality of this lyric is remarkable to have been written by a man, 84 years old.

E.Y. Harburg

Change of Sky

Guess I'll have to go where
moon and stars
Are nowhere there for me
I need a change of sky
I need a change of...

Summer winter spring
Away from every single
memory
The time has come to fly
I need a change of sky

Somewhere, someplace
Where lilacs don't exist
That trembled when we
kissed
In the rain

Some moonless world
Where shadows never part
And daisies shout, "Look out!"
There goes your heart, again
Again, again..

Bless the finders keepers
Kiss the losers weepers
All goodbye

My heart has had it's high
My heart may stay
But I,
I need a change of sky

Somewhere someplace
Where lilacs don't exist
That trembled when we
kissed
In the rain

Some moonless world
Where shadows never part
And daisies shout, "Look out!"
There goes your heart, again
Again, again...

Bless the finders keepers
Kiss the losers weepers
all goodbye
My heart has had it's high
My heart may stay
But I,
I need a change of sky

"In listening to this song, you will hear that Yip again expressed his hope that human beings could live, whatever their color; in love and peace – together."
Philip Springer

7 Love Comes In Many Different Colors

Yip was the only one of my lyric writers who had any real political feelings. The people I wrote with in the Brill Building were interested in baseball; they were not interested in the State of Israel, nor in civil rights in the 50's. So, when I was writing with Buddy Kaye or Joan Javits or Bob Hilliard or Carolyn Leigh or any of the many others, it was not even thought of to discuss politics; I knew that they wouldn't be interested.

But Yip was passionately interested in civil rights. As we all know, "Finian's Rainbow" was the first Broadway musical to feature black people in leading parts.

In listening to this song, you will hear that Yip again expressed his hope that human beings could live, whatever their color; in love and peace - together.

The green grass
The blue sky
The white rose
The red
Give this earth its own
special glow...

The world comes,
The world comes in
Many different colors
This I know!

The blackbird
The bluebird
The red wing
The brown
Give this world its beauty
and grace...

Well when love comes
As life comes
In many different colors
To light up the
Whole human race
The rainbow, the rainbow
Will tie us together
With peace on every face

The blackbird
The bluebird
The red wing
The brown
Give this world its beauty
and grace...

Well when love comes
As life comes
In many different colors
To light up the
Whole human race
The rainbow, the rainbow
Will tie us together
With peace on every face

8 Drivin' and Dreamin'

My brother, artist Anthony Springer, had a role in writing this song. Tony was not a professional songwriter but one of his greatest joys in life was writing songs with me. One day we were improvising, and I, at the piano, came up with this melody. Tony, after hearing the melody, said, "How about the title Drivin' and Dreamin'?"

I played another musical phrase; then he said, "Dreamin' and Drivin'" and I continued with the melody.

That was Tony's key role in the creation of this song and I liked the result enough to take it to Yip. Yip and I never had a third collaborator in working together, so Tony never received credit for his part, but I am giving him credit right now. Without him I never would have written "Drivin' and Dreamin'".

I was truly fortunate to finish the song with Yip and to have my dear friend Alan O'Day, the great rock n' roll writer/singer record this song for me.

Many of Yip's songs throughout his career were dedicated to hopes of a better humanity. This song also had feeling of compassion for those people who were down & out, especially a worker out of a job.

Philip Springer at the piano with his brother, Anthony Springer

24

Drivin' and Dreamin'

Something dies inside a man
When he's on welfare
Makes it hard for him
To face the morning sun

So he tells his kids
There's a job in Eldorado
Not far away
And he'll soon be back
With all their worries gone
With money in his pocket

Drivin' and dreamin'
Dreamin' and drivin'
A man in a beat-up car
Heading for Eldorado
Searching for Shangri-La
Following every rainbow
Drifting from bar to bar

The endless Kansas wheatfields
Make him wonder
Why the cost
Of daily bread
Should be so steep

So he looks up at the stars
For simple answers
They ought to know
But stars and teardrops
never talk
They weep
Better keep on movin'

Drivin' and dreamin'
Dreamin' and drivin'
A man in a beat-up car
Heading for Eldorado
Searching for Shangri-La
Following every rainbow
Drifting from bar to bar

Well he makes it
All the way to California
To a cliff with the Pacific
down below
The waves reflecting
Crazy moving pictures
Was this his life?
He jams the pedal
As far as it can go
Right into the sunset

Drivin' and dreamin'
Dreamin' and drivin'
A man in a beat-up car
Heading for Eldorado
Searching for Shangri-La
Following every rainbow
Maybe some other star

9 Almost

Yip Harburg and Philip Springer. (1980)

"Almost" is the last song I ever wrote with Yip Harburg. We wrote it in the spring of 1980, when our collaboration was in full swing and we were most comfortable writing with each other. Yip came with the title "Almost" and told me the story of two lovers that did not quite make it.

It was the last song that we ever talked about, four days before his death. Yip told me he needed a song to show one of his Hollywood contacts. I suggested "Almost", thinking it was a wonderful song. Yip said, "It's not a great song."

Nonetheless, Yip still wanted to show "Almost" to a major movie producer.

I accepted Yip's evaluation of "Almost", until about 32 years later when I was producing a show called "Trunk Songs". There were twelve singers in the show and everyone wanted to sing that song. I was suddenly hit by the fact that it must be a special song. To get that kind of reaction from the cast was a unique experience for me and during the show the audience seemed to love "Almost". My conclusion is that "Almost" is almost a great song.

Almost

Almost,
We were almost,
One step from heaven's door
We saw the promised land
Walked up hand in hand
And we made it almost

Almost
It was almost
That big time dream come true
The perfect movie plot
Perfect were it not
For that villain, almost
Almost

One of those lovely
Might have been
Could have
Should have been things

Where love glides in on roller skates
Flies out on wings

Pity, what a pity
When love blows up a storm
Why should your golden ship
On a dreamy trip
To the isles of always
Be shipwrecked on the shores
Of almost

10 Crazy Old World

One afternoon, Yip came over to my Pacific Palisades home. When he came in, he saw that I was feeling down and said, "What's lacking here is a little frohlichkeit," which means "happiness" in German.

And then Yip gave me a song title, "Crazy Old World". Since he had asked me to bring happiness to the house, I wrote a very happy tune to that title, "Crazy Old World". Yip went on to write a lyric to my melody and it became one of our most joyful and celebrated collaborations. The song was included in "Somewhere Over the Rainbow: Yip Harburg's America" at the Prince Music Theater in 1999 (as was "Drivin' and Dreamin'").

In 1980 when Yip gave his final concert, he performed a great ensemble version of this song. It brought the packed house down at the distinguished "Lyrics & Lyricists Series" series performance 92nd Street Y in January 1980. These are the words Yip used to introduce the song at that performance:

"But as I said, the population explosion begat other explosions.

Like, suddenly the air became polluted; the milk, diluted. homes uprooted; boys, recruited.

Inflation, rooted; taxes, upbooted;

Pocketbooks, looted; mates ill-suited; sex, disputed."

"All this begat a new kind of music, aided by electronic amplification, beat and noise, so that the violence of our ugly and confused world could be drowned out. What's more, they were displacing the old, romantic, sweet songs. So I decided to come out of the dark rock of ages into the luminous age of rock with a song, composed by Phil Springer at the piano, who you can see by his Mozartian tousled hair, he's a rocker (laughs), which I hope will hit the Top 40 while I'm still in my early 80s. I hope it will be played in all disco shelters, where the bombs can still fall on you but you won't be able to hear them."

"Lyrics & Lyricists Series" performance at the 92nd Street Y in NYC, starring E.Y. Yip Harburg. Composer Philip Springer at the piano. (1980)

Crazy Old World

The prices go up and the
dollar comes down
The heavenly smog rolls over
the town
But the crazy old world keeps
spinning along
And I keep singing my crazy
song

They say it's all gonna end
in a bang
But somehow, I know I'll go
hangin' on

The fish can't swim, and the
birds can't fly
The mushroom cloud floats
merrily by
But the crazy old world keeps
spinnin' around
And I keep makin' my crazy
sound
Echoes of my simple song
Will linger when the whole
thing's long, long gone

Oh, Billy Graham is hawkin'
the hereafter
The Reverend Moon keeps
sellin' me the sky
But the ancient breeze just
rocks the trees with laughter
Ever livin' laughter
While they cry

They've given up
On the human race
Their only hope is outer space
When the eagle crows and
Wall Street cracks
And they all go to heaven
In our Cadillacs
I'll still be finger-pickin'
On my guitar
Pickin' out dreams where
The sweet notes are
In song
While the crazy old world
keeps spinnin', spinnin' along

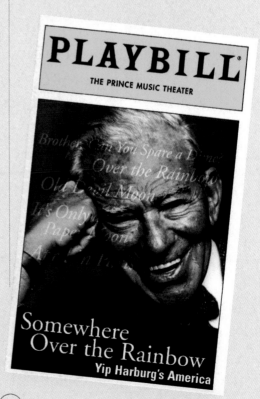

Yip's Last Night

On the evening of March 4th, 1981 at 8 o'clock, Yip came bouncing up my front stairs and burst into the room with flowers and food. We went into the den, where I had a baby grand piano, and did some work together. We spent the rest of the evening with my whole family; my wife and my two daughters, talking and reminiscing. At one point, Yip started speaking in Yiddish and telling us about his childhood in lower Manhattan, in the poorest section.

We talked of many things. He was an admirer of, my daughter Miriam's music; he appreciated her talent. That evening, she played a bit for him, as I did too.

Yip and I worked together at the piano. I played some melodies and Yip recited some poems, spontaneously.

The evening went by and at about 11 o'clock, it was time to part. Yip came to my front door, looked at me with his blue eyes and said, "I'll see you soon Flip", and left down the stairs. The next morning, at about 11:00 a.m., we got a phone call from the lady in whose house Yip had been staying during his visit in L.A. Her words were, "Our friend is no longer with us". Well, my family heard that, both my children started crying, as did my wife, and as did I. That was the end. And so, looking upwards, where Yip is undoubtedly with his yellow pad, trying to find a rhyme for Oz, I say, "I'll see you soon, Yip."

Poem by E.Y. Harburg
Written the night before his death
March 4, 1981

I've blown my little whistle

And banged my little drum

Breathed my little song into the air

And whatever fate awaits me

In that place called Kingdom Come

I'll know the song will still be there

E.Y. "Yip" Harburg

E. Y. "Yip" Harburg (1896-1981), in a career spanning over fifty years, was known as "Broadway's social conscience". A master lyricist, poet and book writer, Yip was always dedicated to social justice. He wrote the words to over 600 songs, most notably, all the lyrics in the 1939 motion picture classic *"The Wizard of Oz"*.

On Broadway, Yip began writing lyrics for multiple revues in the 1930s which included songs that became standards including "Brother, Can You Spare a Dime?", the classic anthem of the Depression (with composer Jay Gorney, 1932) and "April in Paris" (with Vernon Duke, 1932). Among many other works, he co-wrote the book (with Fred Saidy) and wrote the lyrics for *Finian's Rainbow* (1947, music by Burton Lane) which won the Henderson and George Jean Nathan Awards for Best Musical Comedy; for *Flahooley* (1951, music by Sammy Fain), and for *Jamaica*, starring Lena Horne (1957, music by Harold Arlen).

In Hollywood, Yip Harburg wrote lyrics for numerous film musicals during the 1930s and 1940s. His most famous work was *The Wizard of Oz* (1939, with Harold Arlen). In this classic, Yip conceived the integration of song and script, wrote the recitative for the Munchkin "operetta", and wrote the lyrics to all the songs, including the Academy Award-winning "Over the Rainbow". He was also the final script editor and made significant contributions to the dialogue.

Altogether, Yip wrote the lyrics to over 600 songs with a variety of composers. "It's Only a Paper Moon" (1932, with Arlen), "Over the Rainbow" (1939, Harold Arlen), "We're Off to See the Wizard," "Ding Dong! The Witch Is Dead" and "Happiness Is Just a Thing Called Joe" (1943, Arlen, from the film *Cabin in the Sky*). Later, with Lane, he wrote "Old Devil Moon" and "How Are Things in Glocca Morra?"

As Broadway's social commentator, and given his ability to "gild the philosophic pill" with witticisms and a lyric style all his own, Yip Harburg is a unique and major lyricist of 20th century American musical theatre.

Yip Harburg died on March 5, 1981 at 84 years young.

Philip Springer

Philip Springer, born in 1926, is best known for writing the Christmas standard, "Santa Baby", with lyricist Joan Javits, and the Frank Sinatra classic, "How Little it Matters, How Little We Know" with Carolyn Leigh.

"Santa Baby" has been recorded by countless major recording artists, including Madonna, Michael Bublé, Taylor Swift, Ariana Grande, Gwen Stefani, Kelly Pickler, Kylie Minogue, Robbie Williams, R.E.M., Garth Brooks and his wife Trisha Yearwood (featured on their long-awaited Christmas duets album), among many others.

Some of Springer's other notable songs include "The Next Time" by Cliff Richard, lyric Buddy Kaye (No.1 in England); "Moonlight Gambler" by Frankie Laine, lyric Bob Hilliard (Top 10 Billboard); "Heartbroken" by Judy Garland, lyric Fred Ebb; "All Cried Out" by Dusty Springfield, lyric Buddy Kaye; "Never Ending" by Elvis Presley, lyric Buddy Kaye; "Her Little Heart Went to Loveland" by Aretha Franklin, lyric Buddy Kaye.

Springer's first top ten song was "Teasin'" recorded by Connie Haines and, in England, by the Beverly Sisters, lyric Richard Adler.

For several years, Springer wrote songs with Senator Orrin Hatch; Hatch dedicated their song "Headed Home" to Hatch's dear friend, Senator Ted Kennedy.

Springer composed and conducted motion picture scores including "Tell Me That You Love Me, Junie Moon," starring Liza Minelli; "More Dead Than Alive," starring Vincent Price; "I Sailed to Tahiti with an All-Girl Crew," and "Impasse" starring Burt Reynolds. He also scored episodes of the television shows "Gunsmoke", "Mannix", "Along Came Bronson", and "Medical Center" and composed the theme for "Crosswits", a 1970s game show.

Springer composed music for many musical shows, including the off-Broadway musical "The Chosen" based on the best-selling novel by Chaim Potok, in 1988. Songs interpolated in Broadway shows include "Salesmanship" (Ziegfeld Follies of '57; lyric Carolyn Leigh); and You'll Make an Elegant Butler" (Tovarich 1963; lyric Joan Javits) for which he wrote the opening song for Vivien Leigh in her last Broadway performance. Springer wrote a musical, "The Bells of Notre Dame," based on Victor Hugo's epic novel. Tamar Springer will set forth to produce and promote this musical as her next major project.

E. Y. Harburg
551 Fifth Avenue
New York, N. Y. 10017

December 4, 1974

Dear Phil:

        Holt, Rinehart and Winston is pub-
lishing a book about me, my times and rhymes,
my friends and colleagues......and this means
you.

        They want the book to be as candid
and wide-ranging as possible.

        John Lahr is writing it. His asso-
ciates, Bill Weeden and David Finkle will be
calling you for information, insights, anec-
dotes, pictures, or any fol de rol you can
contribute. I will be grateful for your
cooperation in this venture.

        Here is your chance either to
canonize or scandalize.————————

                        This trusting troubadour,

EYH:sb

Mr. Philip Springer
Palisades Park
Los Angeles, Ca.

Recording Dates:

Edelaine	December 1975
Hitchhikers	May 1977
Crazy Old World	January 1980
Time, You Old Gypsy Man	August 1980
Almost	February 1985
Drivin' and Dreamin'	July 1998
It Might Have Been	April 2009
Love Comes in Many Different Colors	July 2010
Change of Sky	April 2018
Wild Red Cherry River	April 2018

The Last Legacy of E.Y. "Yip" Harburg produced by Tamar Springer

Tamar Springer is Philip Springer's younger daughter, and the Executive Director of Tamir Music. Tamar grew up knowing Yip Harburg as a dear family friend and a grandfather figure. Yip made up bedtime stories for Tamar during his visits and she remembers him with a heart full of love.

Mastered by Kevin Lacy

Mixed by Kevin Lacy: It Might Have Been, Wild Red Cherry River
Engineered, mixed and vocal restoration by Kevin Lacy: Hitchhikers

Photos of E.Y. Harburg courtesy of The Estate of E.Y. "Yip" Harburg

Photos of Philip Springer and Anthony Springer courtesy of Tamir Music

All songs co-published by Tamir Music and Glocca Morra Music Corp. (ASCAP)

A project of Good Songs Are Coming Back Records, LLC

www.composerofsantababy.com

SpringerHarburgSongs@gmail.com

© 2021 Tamir Music

All Rights Reserved.

Graphic Design: Steven Messer